Happy Kiddo

Preschool Adventures

Written by Valorie Mathers

Illustrated by Jenni Joyce

Copyright © 2020
All Rights Reserved

This Book Belongs to:

Affirmations

I AM SUPER COOL!
I AM JOY!
I AM UNIQUE!
I AM WORTHY!
I AM CREATIVE!
I AM CLEVER!
I AM BEAUTIFUL!
I AM HEALTHY!
I AM COURAGEOUS!
I AM PEACEFUL!
I AM KINDNESS!
I AM GRATEFUL!
I AM LOVED!

Welcome to the Magical Land of Preschool.
You're a fuzzy little Hedgehog and you're Super Cool.

Say: I am Super Cool!

The drawbridge unfolds and what do I see? So many new friends as joyous as me.

Say: I am Joy!

My new friends are all so different,
We are all unique in our own way.
Some are quiet, some are loud,
And some are ready to go play.

Say: I am Unique!

Now it's time to play,
there's so much to explore.

Lots of toys and fun games
and so much more.

Our teacher created a challenging Maze.
I lead my friends through,
I am worthy of praise.

Say: I am Worthy!

Dance time in the classroom, I can't wait to show my moves.

Music loudly playing, I am creative with my grooves.

Say: I am Creative!

A riddle we must solve to unlock a special treasure.
We all listen, we all know, we must work together.
The answer is something that we must do forever.
Believe in Yourself! We knew it, we are so clever.

Say: I am Clever!

Our treasure opens wide, We peek our heads inside.
Sunshine and glitter so bright, such a beautiful magical sight.

Say: I am Beautiful!

My belly starts to rumble,
It looks like it's time for lunch.
My healthy food's delicious,
My carrots nicely crunch.

Say: I am Healthy!

Time to get up and go outside,
Monkey bars and a great big slide.
This slide is huge, it's outrageous.
I can do this, I am Courageous.

Say: I am Courageous!

Our teacher shows us yoga,
then it's time for meditation.
We help lay out our mats
in the quiet yoga station.

As we stretch so big and bendy,
I feel like an elastic.
My body and mind at one,
so peaceful it's fantastic.

**Say: I am
Peaceful!**

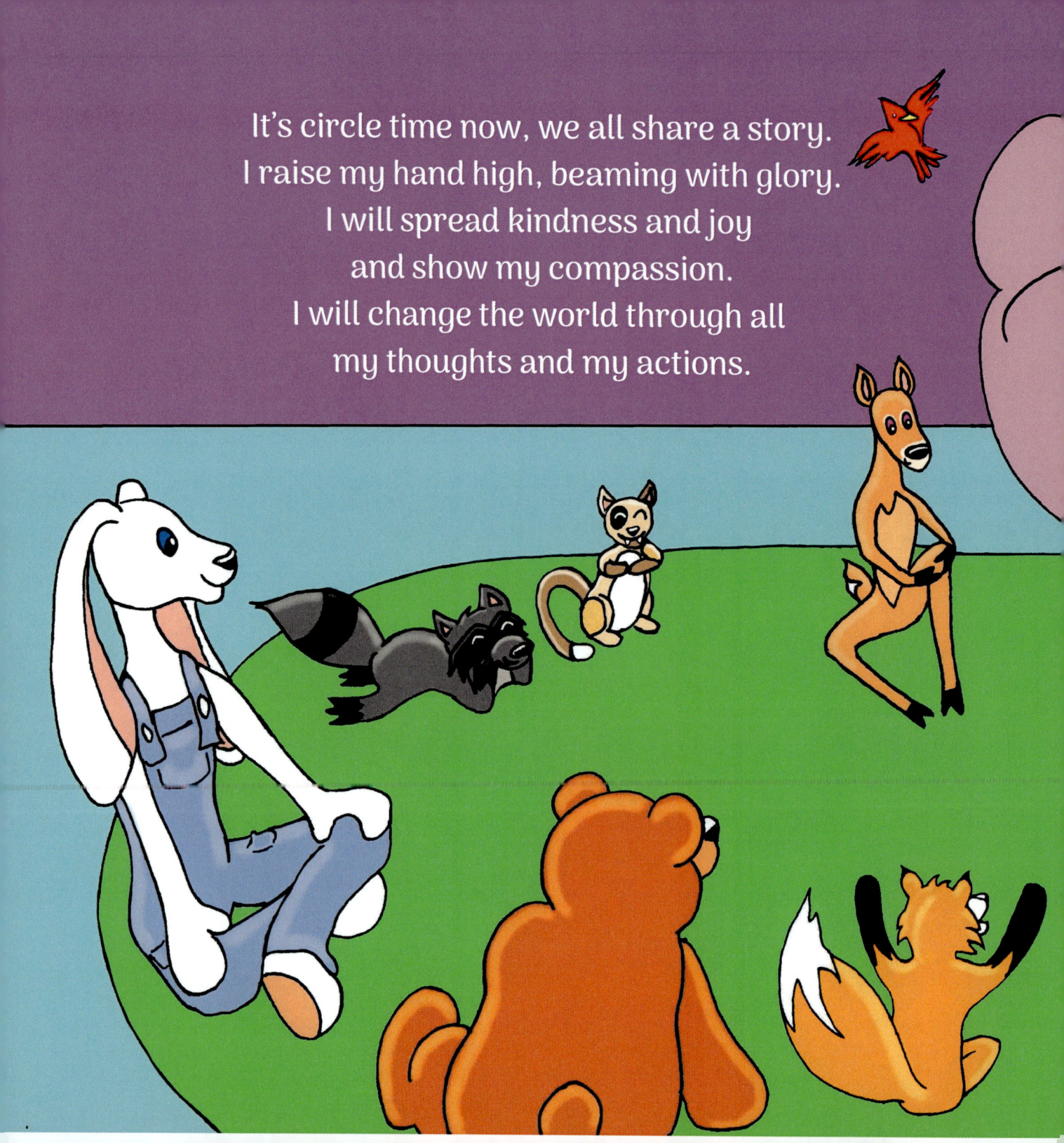

It's circle time now, we all share a story.
I raise my hand high, beaming with glory.
I will spread kindness and joy
and show my compassion.
I will change the world through all
my thoughts and my actions.

Say: I am Kindness!

In this magical land, I had a wonderful day.
I will be back tomorrow, and some more we will play.
My life is amazing, I am so Thankful for that.
With gratitude, I put on my shoes and my hat.

Say: I am Grateful!

The drawbridge unfolds, the sun shines bright through.

My family, great big hugs, they missed me too.

Say: I am Loved!

Affirmations

I AM SUPER COOL!
I AM JOY!
I AM UNIQUE!
I AM WORTHY!
I AM CREATIVE!
I AM CLEVER!
I AM BEAUTIFUL!
I AM HEALTHY!
I AM COURAGEOUS!
I AM PEACEFUL!
I AM KINDNESS!
I AM GRATEFUL!
I AM LOVED!

I AM ⟫————————⟪ !
I AM ⟫————————⟪ !
I AM ⟫————————⟪ !
I AM ⟫————————⟪ !
I AM ⟫————————⟪ !

Happy Kiddo Books

Publishing Co.

happykiddobooks.ca

Made in the USA
Las Vegas, NV
22 March 2025

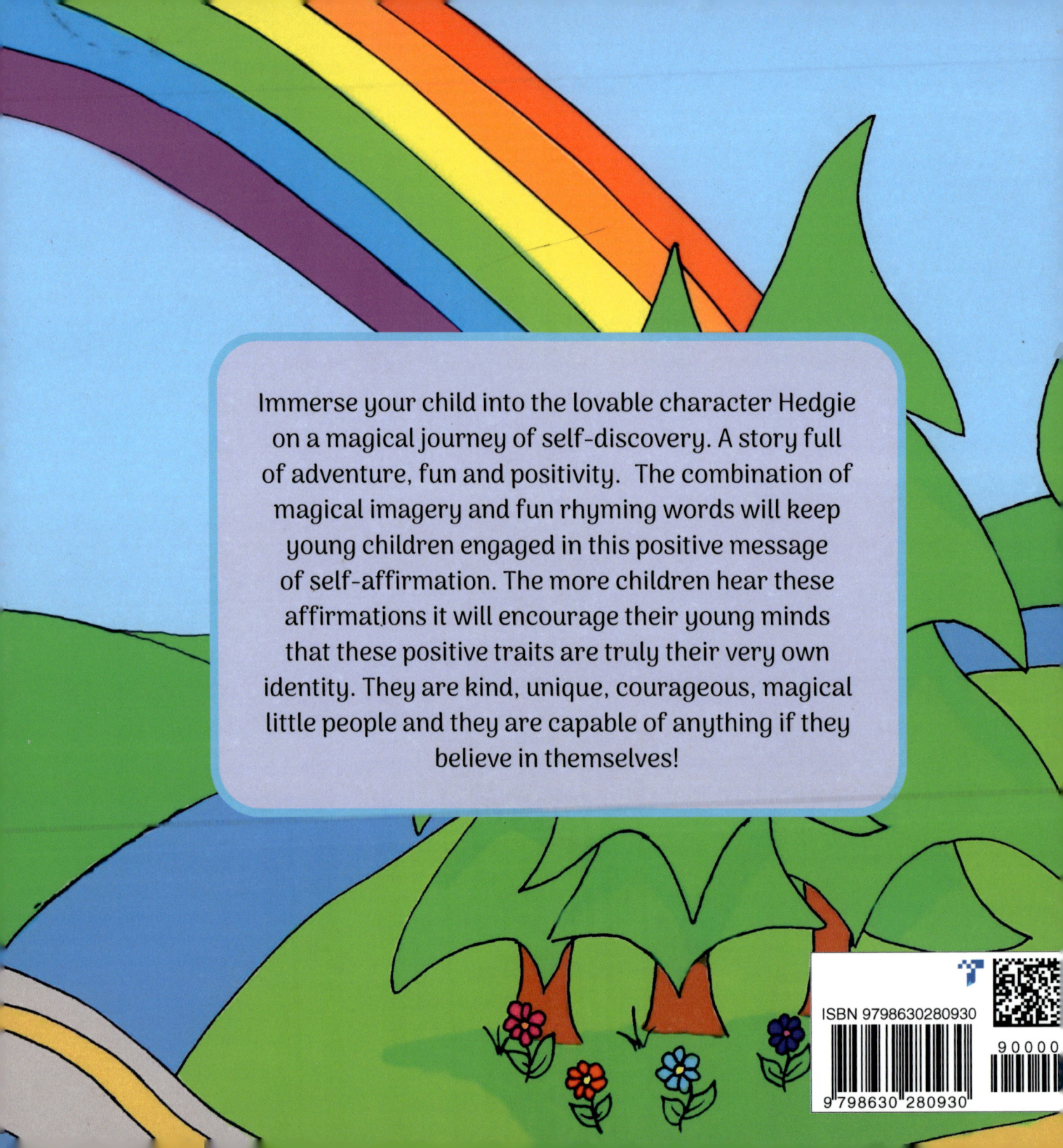

Immerse your child into the lovable character Hedgie on a magical journey of self-discovery. A story full of adventure, fun and positivity. The combination of magical imagery and fun rhyming words will keep young children engaged in this positive message of self-affirmation. The more children hear these affirmations it will encourage their young minds that these positive traits are truly their very own identity. They are kind, unique, courageous, magical little people and they are capable of anything if they believe in themselves!

ISBN 9798630280930